WEDGWOOD WARE

Monographs on Pottery and Porcelain
Edited by W. B. HONEY

C. LILAC JASPER-WARE TEAPOT. MARK, 'WEDGWOOD'
LATE EIGHTEENTH CENTURY
Victoria and Albert Museum.   See pages 14, 16

WEDGWOOD WARE

by

W. B. HONEY

Keeper of the Department of Ceramics
Victoria and Albert Museum
London

FABER AND FABER
24 Russell Square
London

First published in mcmxlviii
by Faber and Faber Limited
24 Russell Square London W.C. 1
Second Impression mcmli
Printed in Great Britain by
R. MacLehose and Company Limited
The University Press Glasgow
Colour plates printed by
Fine Art Engravers Limited, Esher

To

THE HONOURABLE JOSIAH WEDGWOOD

FOREWORD

In choosing and discussing these masterpieces of Wedgwood ware I have wished to present the different sides of the great potter's work in corrected proportion and perspective. Thus I have for the first time given due prominence to the wares with coloured glazes, which Wedgwood made for more than ten years at Burslem; and I have particularly stressed the importance of his part in developing the cream-coloured ware from the earlier Staffordshire types. All these were on the main road of English ceramic evolution, while the decorative stonewares with which the name of Wedgwood is most often associated took but a by-path. The world-wide success of his cream-coloured pottery, which everywhere supplanted the usual *faïence* or delftware, was in fact an event of far-reaching significance, the implications of which are still being worked out by his descendants today in many beautiful new types of pottery. These too are for the first time fully represented in an account of Wedgwood ware, so that this book, unlike the others in its series, is concerned with the present and future as much as with the past.

W. B. H.

ACKNOWLEDGEMENT

The thanks of the author are due to the owners of specimens for permission to reproduce them here, and to the Director and Secretary of the Victoria and Albert Museum for the use of photographs. Grateful acknowledgement is also made to the staff of Messrs. Josiah Wedgwood & Sons Ltd. for information gladly given.

CONTENTS

ILLUSTRATIONS
COLOUR PLATES

MONOCHROME PLATES

PLATES

xiv

PLATES

THE SIGNIFICANCE OF WEDGWOOD

It is generally agreed that Josiah Wedgwood, founder of the great manufactory at Etruria in Staffordshire, was the most influential and significant single figure in the history of English pottery. He was the only Englishman ever to enjoy a European reputation as a potter; he set a Continental as well as an English fashion, and established a technical tradition that has lasted to this day. But that he was the greatest English potter is by no means so unanimously agreed. It is even denied that he was an artist at all. His epitaph in the churchyard at Stoke-on-Trent makes the claim for him that he 'converted a rude and inconsiderable Manufactory into an elegant Art and an important part of National Commerce'; but a leading Continental historian of pottery, Emil Hannover, has contradicted this, saying that Wedgwood found an art, rude and inconsiderable perhaps, and transformed it to its great loss into a manufacture; while another critic, an Englishman, has lately spoken of 'the baleful figure of Wedgwood . . . confining the native English genius for pottery in the strait-jacket of Neo-Classicism'.

Some of this present-day coolness towards Wedgwood's reputation is no doubt due to reaction against the uncritical enthusiasm of the nineteenth century and the fulsome adulation of Wedgwood's Victorian biographer, who was as much concerned to affirm her admiration for his 'character', and illustrate his disapproval of 'every kind of moral laxity', as to determine his rank as an artist-manufacturer. But while some of this disparagement may be justified, most of it is due to misunderstanding and a narrowness of vision. Wedgwood was an instrument, even a prophet, of the Industrial Revolution. Already by his time the machine had begun to replace hand labour in many departments of industry, and the standardising and purifying of ingredients and the economical division of labour had aimed at reducing production costs and the elimination of all chance variations in the ware. Wedgwood himself, employing every known improvement in methods of manufacture and inventing others himself, was responsible for many technical advances; he was constantly concerned to secure a modern efficiency and economy in both process and productions. In all this he was perhaps engineer, chemist, organiser, reformer and business man, rather than potter and artist. But he was none the less a great man and a benefactor of humanity.

*   *   *

So far as Wedgwood was an artist or man of taste at all he showed a vision severely limited by the narrow fashions of his day. The revived-Classical movement of the second half of the eighteenth century possessed him absolutely.

This Neo-Classical movement is often explained as the result of the excavation of Pompeii and Herculaneum and the publication of their finds there by Sir William Hamilton, the Comte de Caylus and others. But much was due to an inevitable reaction, to a revolt against the late Baroque and Rococo extravagance of the middle decades of the eighteenth century. It was as much a return to simplicity as a rediscovery of the ancient world, and was claimed to be 'rational' in its return to symmetry after an orgy of *chinoiseries* and fantastic Rococo ornament. It was even 'scientific' since it proposed yet another 'return to nature'. Such 'pure' and 'correct' taste (as it was claimed to be), constantly striving after 'elegance', would have been dully academic at any other time; but in the late-eighteenth century it glowed with the fire of the current admirations and rediscoveries. It had vitality at the time, however thin-blooded it may appear at first sight to a generation knowing it only in a hundred weak derivatives. But to claim it as the only 'pure' taste, as is still sometimes done (in America, particularly) is of course absurd. It is noteworthy too that the English Neo-Classical is charged with a peculiar sweetness of sentiment which distinguishes it from the Greco-Roman art from which it was so largely copied and is of course far removed from the taut astringent quality of authentic Greek art itself. Not only were the subjects of the decoration sentimentalised in expression and treatment, but the Classical shapes themselves, of urn and amphora and the rest, were altered and exaggerated with a similar result.

Such then, was the Neo-Classical style, with its decoration of swags and garlands, its cameo-medallions and reclining figures, in the embodiment of which in pottery Wedgwood became an acknowledged leader, so that even the great Continental porcelain-factories were compelled to imitate him. He did not himself create the style, but to the extent to which he adopted it he was a pioneer and reformer in matters of taste as well as of technique and organisation.

Wedgwood's influence in this was on the whole of benefit to the potter's art at the time, though seen in perspective, with the background of earlier ceramic achievement clearly in view, it may well appear disastrous. Besides pruning away all the delightful Rococo extravagance of the porcelain-makers and the *chinoiseries* of the delftware, with its unpractical but sympathetic material, he aimed at an ideal which denied most of the ceramic virtues. Though himself a skilled pottery-craftsman, he seemed to have no clay-sense, and in all his fashionable work he sought by a vain imitation of stone and metal to conceal its origin in clay. Such direct and vital plastic shapes as those of the English medieval ware (for example) he would have considered intolerably 'rude'. In decoration too he favoured a timid neatness and elegance, an exaggerated English 'sobriety' and 'good taste', rather than the freedom and vitality of which the pottery-painter's brush is capable. Neither the breadth and swift power of the Italians nor the easy careless grace of the incomparable Marseilles *faïence* (for example) would have satisfied his standard of beauty and correctness. Even the art of the porcelain-painter, of the miniaturist in enamels, was apparently outside his comprehension, since the only important instance of his using it, done to the order of the Empress Catherine II of Russia, was artistically a failure. Despising the 'gaudiness' of the usual porcelain-decoration he had that famous 'Russian service' painted in a dingy and supposedly 'Classical' purple-black, applied on many pieces with a laboured insignificance that left it unworthy of comparison with its predecessors in the porcelain he hoped to rival and replace.

Nor was his positive achievement with his new decorative materials much greater. These he had produced as more worthy of his ideals, but the use he made of them, for all its exquisite workmanship, was essentially non-ceramic; the decoration applied to his black basaltes, jasper ware, and the rest, was directly inspired by cameo carving in gem-stones, and though this relief decoration was immensely popular in his own day, and is still largely made for the provincial and American markets, this part of Wedgwood's work cannot be regarded as anything but a *cul-de-sac*, aside from the main road of English ceramic evolution. It was a by-way comparable, in its origin in a fashion, with the modern artist-potters' imitation of early Chinese stoneware. Both were the result of an overmastering admiration claiming an absolute pre-eminence for the period chosen for emulation. Nevertheless Wedgwood's own work on this side maintained an exceedingly high standard in fineness of material and in quality of workmanship. Much of this can be appreciated only when a piece is held in the hand, but even photographs can show something of the excitedly delicate and 'living' touch of the tool used in finishing the reliefs.

*   *   *

But the disparagement (as it may seem) of the foregoing paragraphs is really quite beside the point, since Wedgwood's decorative wares, though the more familiar part of his productions, were only a small and in the strict sense of the word insignificant part of his full achievement. His chief work, viewed in the light of history, is to be found in his useful wares for the table, made for the most part in plain cream-coloured earthenware. This in its refined form was virtually his own creation—a dense hard efficient ware, more practical in use than the soft-bodied and absorbent but charming tin-glazed delftware or *faïence*, which it quickly superseded everywhere. In it his disregard of what we call clay quality became a positive merit. As already suggested, Wedgwood (like some of his ablest successors) was an organiser, engineer and chemist rather than an artist, and his contribution to the development of pottery in England was mainly technical; and the kind of art his useful wares foreshadowed, with their simplicity and functional efficiency in use and the economy and precision of their making, was something entirely new and in the highest degree significant. They implied a revolution still in process of fulfilment by Wedgwood's successors in our own day.

Broadly considered, this revolution led to the familiar substitution of handicraft by the machine, and the replacement of the craftsman designing his own work by the external artist designing for massproduction. The change had of course already started before Wedgwood began. The process of pottery casting, for instance, introduced a decade or so before his time, allowed the rapid multiplication of a form, and this, with the use of the lathe, brought a new and mechanical precision to shapes which had previously shown the organic freedom and irregularity of handwork. The consequences of these changes were two-fold, and are shared by all other mechanised industrial arts at the present day: on the one hand the machine by cheapening production brought amenities within the reach of a great many people for whom the cost of hand-made goods was prohibitive; and on the other, an entirely new type of design was created, or at any rate called for. Wedgwood's economies in production were not, it is true, primarily directed towards cheapness; they were to him the means of providing a finer and finer quality of ware for the fashionable market which had previously bought porcelain and was now to be persuaded to buy earthenware. But a much larger market was from the first made possible.

As regards the design of these wares it is remarkable that the word should be capable of so wide an application as to cover both the freehand creation of form by a craftsman, and the imposing of a shape, mechanically reproduced and multiplied, in the way that is now normal in a modern factory. To those for whom aesthetic merit depends on organic irregularity in a form which is the product of an artist's often unselfconscious sensibility, working in collaboration with a material, design of the latter type cannot produce a work of art at all. But the arts of architecture and printing are instances enough to show that in the one case form imposed by an external designer taking no physical part in production may achieve the status of a work of art; while in the other the mechanical multiplication of a design is a commonplace. Both books and buildings are accepted as works of art. Mass-production gives in fact the opportunity for a new sort of aesthetic achievement.

Such a machine-art will obey none of the laws governing the handicraft it replaces, and tradition in the sense of method and skill will obviously be interrupted by it; though clay is employed both in throwing a pot and in casting it, a different order of invention is required for each, and the experience of the artist-potter becomes almost worthless in the factory. But the tradition that resides in a national or local preference for certain types of form may still be felt as a beneficial influence. It will, for example, dictate the rejection of bizarre and self-consciously original 'modernistic' shapes, and ensure a 'native commonsense' and efficiency in use; and with the English tradition in this sense Wedgwood was closely in touch. Here he was a pioneer on the main road of English ceramic progress and his achievement was very great indeed. He was in effect the prophet of a new age in both the technical and the social and economic senses. The change to factory methods has been widely deplored as the invasion by commercialism of a field where standards of good workmanship and ideals of service had previously been accepted. But the accusation confuses the potentially beneficial machine with the commercialism that exploits it for profit. To save labour cannot fail to be of benefit to the community as a whole, in a world where a living has always been desperately hard to get, while the new methods bring their own new order of beauty. The supersession of handicraft in some departments of pottery-making may be regrettable, but it is inevitable; for it is certain that handicraft could be brought back to its former place (apart from sentimental revivals lacking economic reality) only by a complete break-down of Western civilisation.

*　　　*　　　*

Wedgwood's successors, after marking time for more than a century, have in recent years made great advances in the direction indicated by his innovations. Not only have they frankly, and with a kind of symbolical fitness, accepted the parallel of architecture by employing an architect-designer, but in the field of decoration they have shown a clear-sighted understanding of the essential principles of mechanical production. Painting on pottery obviously had no important place in the first Josiah Wedgwood's conception of the art; his use of slight painting of foliate borders and Classical garlands called for none of the skill and bold freedom shown in earlier periods in the history of pottery. In the nineteenth century the tradition of pottery-painting, never very strongly rooted in England, was plainly almost dead. Lithographic transfers giving a facsimile reproduction of painting in full colours were widely used, and even where the brush was employed, transfer-printed outlines robbed the operation of all spontaneity. Only simple sprig patterns, indeed, were within the competence of the factory hands, and when the division of labour eventually made these the work of several persons, each adding a touch or two in one colour only, the pretence that this was pottery-painting was finally reduced to absurdity. But there existed already an appropriate medium of decoration, a medium which had indeed been employed by the first Josiah Wedgwood in the eighteenth century, though fallen out of fashion. Transfer-printing in linear designs made and multiplied by means of an engraved metal plate, could provide an entirely satisfactory autographic reproduction of an artist's own touch and style. Like the printing of books, the transfer-printing of designs on pottery has a special fitness in modern mass-production. Given in the designer a sympathetic understanding of the potter's processes, and in the manufacturer a respect for the artist's vision and integrity, the technique should provide much apt and delightful decoration on pottery in the future. But it must be printing in its own right, so to speak, not tied to a tedious reproduction of painting, but frankly linear or stippled work.

Hitherto the Wedgwood firm has been concerned only with the standardised fine products of a factory. The work of the artist-potter, with his free creation of thrown shapes and his more or less experimental glazes, belongs, as I have explained, to quite another world. Yet both use clay and practise arts of form. Now while it is no longer economically possible, or even desirable, to employ the artist-potter to make articles of everyday use, which the factory can make so much more efficiently, there is nevertheless a profound need and longing for his work, which alone can give a satisfaction comparable to that given by painting and sculpture. The artist exercises, and calls for in his patron, a tactile and visual sensibility and judgement of quality which the factory-made wares can never satisfy, for all their clean, hard and calculated perfection. The artist-potter's activity is in this way in a sense complementary to that of the factory. Given his full freedom and not mistakenly expected to design shapes for multiplication, such an artist might well serve as a kind of research worker to the factory, not so much in the scientific sense (since his methods are so different), as in what might be called the exploration of the aesthetic possibilities of a living ceramic art. Such a complementary activity has been found possible, and worth while, at some modern Continental factories, and it is perhaps not presumptuous to hope that room may be found for it within the wide limits of modern Barlaston.

2

THE WORK OF THE
FIRST JOSIAH WEDGWOOD (1730-95)

Josiah Wedgwood was born in 1730, at Burslem in Staffordshire, one of the Five Towns now federated to form the county-borough of Stoke-on-Trent and known as 'the Potteries'. He was the thirteenth child of Thomas Wedgwood, and at the age of nine, on the death of his father, he began work in the family pottery, known as the Churchyard Pottery, then become the property of his eldest brother Thomas, to whom he was in 1744 apprenticed for five years. At the end of this period he joined Thomas Alders, a potter at Stoke, in partnership with a tradesman named Harrison, making 'agate', 'black', 'tortoiseshell' and salt-glazed wares of the contemporary Staffordshire kinds. This partnership probably came to an end about 1752, and in 1754 Wedgwood joined Thomas Whieldon of Fenton Low, devoting himself to the improvement of the wares with coloured glazes, and in 1759, having produced a finer green glaze and having now sufficient capital, started manufacturing on his own account in the Ivy House, Burslem, making all sorts of pottery of the so-called Whieldon types, including salt-glazed stoneware, which are now hardly distinguishable from the wares of his contemporary Staffordshire potters. Improving the cream-coloured ware and eventually securing the patronage of Queen Charlotte he extended his business greatly, and in 1764 took over larger premises in the neighbouring Brick House Works, afterwards known as the Bell House.

In 1762 Wedgwood met at Liverpool a merchant named Thomas Bentley, who inspired him with a love of the antique and with whom as partner in 1768 he proceeded with the building of a new factory, house and village, on the Ridge House estate, two miles from Burslem, which he named Etruria. (Most Greek vases were at that time believed to be Etruscan.) These premises were finished and occupied in the following year. The partnership with Bentley related to the manufacture of vases and ornamental wares only; the 'useful wares' continued to be made at the Bell House under the direction of Josiah's cousin Thomas Wedgwood, until about 1771–73, when the workmen and plant were gradually removed to Etruria.

A. 'TORTOISESHELL' EARTHENWARE PLATE
ABOUT 1760
Schreiber Collection. *See pages* 8, 9

Wedgwood's first efforts at the new factory were directed towards the improvement of the Staffordshire unglazed black earthenware, to make a fine stoneware which he called 'black basaltes' and used at first for imitations of Greek vases; and towards the improvement of the various kinds of marbled ware which had been made at Burslem. Then followed a search for new materials. He particularly wanted a ware in which to make white relief decoration on coloured grounds in the style of carved cameos in such semi-precious stone as layered onyx; and his 'jasper ware' (as he called it) was perfected for this purpose about 1774–75. Bentley died in 1780. In 1790 Wedgwood's sons John, Josiah and Thomas, and his nephew Thomas Byerley were taken into partnership, making the firm 'Josiah Wedgwood, Sons and Byerley'; three years later it consisted of Wedgwood, his son Josiah and Byerley alone. In 1795 Wedgwood died, having secured a world-wide market for his productions and those of his fellow Staffordshire potters.

'Cauliflower' and 'pineapple' wares, and other earlier Staffordshire types: Wedgwood's first productions, made at Burslem in the period of nearly ten years before the building of Etruria, and for a few years after, were undoubtedly similar to those of his former partner Thomas Whieldon, and are difficult to identify separately (1). The name of Whieldon is commonly attached only to a deep-cream-coloured earthenware with glaze mottled and stained with green, grey, black, brown, blue and yellow, often called 'tortoiseshell ware'. But excavations on the site of his pottery at Fenton Low have shown him to have made all the Staffordshire types of the early industrial period— unglazed red teapots of the so-called Elers type, glazed red and white earthenware (the so-called Astbury ware), 'solid agate', the black-glazed ware often erroneously attributed to Jackfield, and grey and white salt-glazed stoneware, as well as the mottled ware. Wedgwood's improved green and yellow glazes made possible the now-well-known vessels in the form of cauliflowers and pineapples (2). His productions in this period differed from those of his contemporaries chiefly in their finer finish, due to his attention to detail and to the standardisation of shapes and materials. Some wares with reliefs of landscapes, said to have been modelled for Wedgwood by William Greatbach (3), some green and gilt wares with applied reliefs (4), striped and fluted wares (5), and some nearly plain pieces with impressed dots (6), all show the new and improved glazes with excellent effect. Fragments of similar ware were, it is said, found on the site of the Ivy House works, and a 'black tortoiseshell' tea-caddy in the Victoria and Albert Museum with

(1) *Plates* 1 to 13; *Colour-Plate* A; (2) *Plates* 8, 9; (3) *Plate* 3; (4) *Plate* 11; (5) *Plate* 6; (6) *Plate* 1.

a *chinoiserie* design (1) actually bears the mark 'Wedgwood'. 'Agate ware' knife handles and salt-glazed stoneware are known to have been made, and 'blocks' or patrices for some of the latter are still preserved at the Wedgwood Works Museum; a cornucopia-shaped flower-holder with a relief emblematical of Plenty (2), and plates and dishes with basketwork borders (3) are included. These were made both in salt-glaze and in 'Whieldon' earthenware (4), like the popular 'sprigged' ware (5). Green-glazed wares with leaves in moulded relief have continued to be made to the present day (6).

Cream-coloured earthenware: This ware, so familiar to-day, was largely the creation of Josiah Wedgwood. Refining the Whieldon cream body, which had been made whiter and harder by the use of calcined flint, Wedgwood became the leader of a movement shared by the Leeds and other factories, by which the English cream-coloured ware replaced the customary tin-glazed *faïence* or delftware in well-to-do markets all over the world. The ware was refractory enough, on account of the flint, to be fired to stoneware hardness and partial vitrification and this was eventually increased by the use in it of a pro-portion of Cornish china-stone. The right to do this, in spite of the porcelain-patent held by Richard Champion of Bristol, was re-affirmed as regards wares that were not translucent, at the time of Champion's application for the renewal of his patent in 1775. The lead-glaze of the cream-coloured ware was hard, but not as hard as the salt-glaze of the earlier Staffordshire type, which will abrade a silver spoon! The perfected ware was variously known abroad as *faïence fine*, *Steingut*, *Engels-porseleyn*, and *flint-porslin*. After securing the patronage of Queen Charlotte, Wedgwood at some undetermined date (perhaps as early as 1765) named it 'Queen's ware'. In a letter of 1767 he spoke of 'cream-coloured, alias Queen's ware', suggesting that the name had not then been long in use.

In or soon after 1779, Wedgwood introduced a fine pure-white glazed earthenware which he named 'pearl ware'; in this the cream tinge (due apparently to traces of iron in the lead-glaze) was counter-acted by a minute quantity of cobalt blue. It was sometimes trans-lucent on account of the considerable proportion of china-stone it contained, and this was humorously lamented by Wedgwood, in a letter to Bentley, as an inadvertent infringement of Champion's patent rights. The 'pearl-ware' was chiefly used for tea-services made in rivalry with porcelain. Porcelain or china in the accepted sense of the words was never made by the first Josiah Wedgwood.

---

(1) Compare *Plate* 2; (2) *Plate* 13; (3) *Plates* 4, 5, *Colour-Plate* A; (4) *Plates* 10, 12; (5) *Plate* 7; (6) compare *Plate* 85A.

CREAM-COLOURED WARE

The perfected cream-colour was used for table wares, kitchen and dairy equipment, and household utensils of every sort (1), to the forms of which Wedgwood paid great attention, improving their efficiency in such details as spouts, handles and lids. Tiles are said to have been first made about 1769, and very large plaques were successfully fired in 1776. The portrait- and animal-painter George Stubbs, requiring large plaques of cream-coloured ware for enamel-painting, induced his friend Wedgwood to manufacture these, which represent a considerable technical achievement. A panel three feet high with a portrait by Stubbs of the potter himself, dated 1782, is in the Lady Lever Art Gallery, Port Sunlight.

The shapes employed at first followed the Staffordshire rustic style, with 'cabbage-leaf' spouts and twisted, notched and 'crabstock' handles (2). In these early wares the material was often a deep cream-colour, but the attribution to Wedgwood is sometimes uncertain. Next, a beautiful restrained Rococo was taken up, probably inspired by French *faïence*, with wavy shell-like forms picked out in green or purple (3). With the increasing adoption of the Classical manner, shapes became plainer and plainer, with lobed and shell edges as a last concession to the outgoing style (4). The Classical forms had prevailed by about 1775, as is shown by the first catalogue of the Queen's ware, issued by Wedgwood about that time. This was illustrated by nine pages of engravings showing the forms of plates, etc., and another of an elaborate centre-piece with pierced decoration and hanging baskets. Decoration in the clay was thenceforward almost confined to beaded and feather-edged borders and pierced openwork (5). Shapes were much influenced by the austere and graceful design of the contemporary silver. The Wedgwood styles were to a large extent shared with Leeds, from which the earlier, unmarked, wares are sometimes distinguished with difficulty. Leeds often has a very low foot-ring and a greenish-toned glaze, while Wedgwood plates are rounded beneath, without foot-ring, and the ware was latterly harder-looking and of a pale ivory or cream colour; but the colour of both varied widely. The catalogues issued by Wedgwood, Leeds, Castleford, and other firms sometimes help to place a specimen, but there was much copying.

Painted decoration on the earliest cream-colour is often of disputed origin, like the ware itself. Some unidentified painting is recorded to have been done outside the factory by a Mrs. Warburton of Hot Lane, Cobridge, amongst others, and some rather rustic but admirably vital

---

(1) *Plates* 16 to 41; (2) *Plates* 16, 17, 18; (3) *Plates* 23A, 25; (4) *Plate* 24; (5) *Plates* 20, 31.

decoration of landscapes and figures in bright enamel colours and pink lustre, was perhaps their work. Designs of plough and wheatsheaves ('Speed the Plough'), stylised flowers mainly in red and black, and chintz and scale patterns and ingenious formal designs, usually on a deep cream ground, are among the most beautiful types of the period about 1765–75 (1). There is no actual proof that even the ware is Wedgwood's (though the shapes are often his), but it is unlikely that as much of it is Leeds as is generally claimed. Decorators in Leeds named Robinson and Rhodes are recorded as enamelling salt-glaze in the 1760's, and some of this red-and-black painting also may perhaps be their work; it is tempting to conjecture a connection between this Rhodes and the David Rhodes, also a Yorkshireman, later employed by Wedgwood in London. The red-and-black style is of course not at all in Wedgwood's own taste.

Slight borders of laurel foliage and berries, husk-pattern, and other Classical motives (2) soon became the only painted decoration on the typical Wedgwood cream-colour. This was, however, sensitively neat and graceful, and its sparingness showed to full advantage the fine colour and hard smooth even glaze of the ware. Occasionally more elaborate painting was done, especially in the Wedgwood and Bentley period. In 1768 the enameller David Rhodes was employed in London, first at Great Newport Street and afterwards at Chelsea, where a branch under Bentley's supervision was opened in 1769. The enormous service of nearly a thousand pieces ordered by the Empress Catherine II of Russia in 1773 (the so-called Frog Service) was somewhat laboriously painted at Chelsea under Bentley's direction with named English landscapes and country houses in purplish black (3). From the earliest Burslem days, use was made of transfer-printed decoration, the wares being sent on pack-horses to Sadler and Green at Liverpool. An account of 1764 shows this work already considerable. The prints, though not always well placed on the piece, were generally engraved with taste and skill in the styles popularised by Hancock of Worcester (4). The printing was sometimes coloured over, as in a most attractive pattern of shells and fishes obviously inspired by Marseilles *faïence* (5). Transfer-printing continued to be done outside the factory until 1805, though the outlines of shields and crests were sometimes printed at Etruria before that date.

Vases in cream-coloured ware and marbled ware: It was Wedgwood's desire, from the moment he became aware of the Classical revival, to make vases in the style of the antique. These he made at first, in his

---

(1) *Plates* 16, 17; (2) *Plates* 32 to 40; (3) *Plate* 41; (4) *Plates* 24, 26 to 31; (5) *Plate* 25B.

B. AGATE-WARE VASE. MARK, 'WEDGWOOD & BENTLEY'
ABOUT 1775
Victoria and Albert Museum.   See page 12

Burslem period, in cream-coloured ware, decorating them with lathe-cut bands ('engine-turning') (1) and restrained enamelling and gilding, or by marbling or speckling the surface with coloured glazes or slips, sometimes in the manner of the 'Whieldon' type with applied reliefs (2), but more often in deliberate imitation of natural stones (3). Wedgwood's experience in making 'agate' ware at Ivy House served him in good stead when making at a later date his more ambitious vases by the same method of mingling clays of different colours (4). These vases, variously known as 'marbled', 'agate', 'onyx', 'crystalline', and 'pebbled', include some of Wedgwood's most characteristic and important work. The use here of a lathe is important in view of its modern development; Wedgwood is in fact stated to have installed an engine-turning-lathe at Burslem as early as 1763.

Black basaltes, red, and cane-coloured stonewares: Wedgwood's desire to make vases was inspired or strongly influenced by the contemporary admiration for the Greek pottery then called Etruscan, and attempts to imitate this were naturally soon made by him.

Seeking a suitable material he turned for the purpose to one of the less important local Staffordshire types, the unglazed 'black Egyptian ware' which had been used occasionally for teapots and table-wares. Improving and refining this, he produced about 1767 the first specimens of what he named 'black basaltes', a very hard, fine-grained stoneware, capable of being polished on the lapidary's wheel. It was described by Wedgwood himself as 'a fine black porcelaine having nearly the same properties as the basaltes, resisting the attacks of acids, being a touchstone to copper, silver and gold, and equal in hardness to agate or porphyry.' Its texture was such that it took on a dull gloss with a very slight rubbing. It was at once used for vases, a few of which were 'bronzed' with lightly fired metallic gold, while others were painted (probably at the Chelsea workshop) with red and white mat-surfaced 'encaustic' enamels in lifeless imitation of the ancient Greek vases (5); both the 'bronze Etruscan' and the 'painted Etruscan' date from 1769 onwards. A series of life-sized busts of Classical and modern authors, for library decoration (6), and some large figures of Tritons and Sphinxes were among the more important earlier productions in basaltes (1770 onwards). A figure of Voltaire (7) dates from 1777. The decoration in relief on vases was at first limited to fluting and engine-turning of various kinds (8). Separately moulded and applied low-relief ornament was not successfully used on the curved surface of vases until about 1775, but the identity of material

---

(1) *Plate* 42; (2) *Plate* 44; (3) *Plates* 43, 45; (4) *Plates* 46, 47, *Colour-Plate* B; (5) *Plates* 50 to 53; (6) *Plate* 54; (7) *Plate* 55; (8) *Plate* 57.

in body and reliefs lessened the difficulty of unequal contraction which at a later period delayed the production of white reliefs on a coloured body; and flat plaques with cameo reliefs, all in black basaltes, were produced as early as 1769. Some of these, however, were moulded in one piece. The processes of applying reliefs to very large tablets was not mastered until 1776. Besides the vases, pedestals, busts, half-figures for architectural use, seals and plaques and portrait-medallions, all kinds of useful wares (tea-services, inkstands, flower-pots, etc.) were made in the black basaltes (1). Many of the smaller reliefs were made to gratify the taste, current in the latter part of the eighteenth and early nineteenth centuries, of collecting cameos in cabinets. When originals could not be afforded, copies in glass-paste, red sulphur, and even plaster, were collected, and to this class belonged the Wedgwood copies (2), which could not of course be compared in fineness of grain with their ancient and Renaissance originals in semi-precious stone.

The unglazed red stoneware was not as popular with Wedgwood, reminding him, as he said, of red teapots (though these had laid the foundations of Staffordshire prosperity). It had formed part of the Burslem productions, dating at the latest from 1763. The 'rose-engine-turned' table-wares in this material (3), often marked with imitation Chinese characters and sometimes erroneously ascribed to the Elers brothers, are in many cases of Wedgwood's manufacture. With the introduction of basaltes the same styles and designs were applied to the red ware, which was then called 'rosso antico' (4). Buff ('cane-colour') and biscuit-coloured stonewares were also used in the same way; and enamel decoration was occasionally added to them (5).

Jasper-ware: Wedgwood's search for a fine white stoneware suitable for reliefs resulted first in the production of a semi-porcelain of pale straw or brownish biscuit colour or greyish-toned white, and finally in the invention about 1774–75 of the famous ware which he named 'jasper'. This was a material containing a novel ingredient in barium sulphate, obtained in the form of a mineral from Derbyshire known as 'cawk'. By the end of 1775 this 'jasper' stoneware had been made in blue and sea-green as well as white, and was immediately applied to the making of cameos and seals. By an early improvement, dictated by difficulties in the firing, which was apt to give a spotted effect, and by the high price of the colouring oxides, the tint of the ground was given by a wash only of the coloured jasper, producing what was known as 'jasper dip'. This was invented in 1777 and became usual after

---

(1) *Plates* 56 to 61; (2) *Plate* 59A; (3) *Plate* 14; (4) *Plate* 15; (5) *Plates* 62, 63.

about 1780. Sometimes a laminated effect was desired, as in some gem-stones. The colours eventually used included a dark blue, the familiar light blue or lavender, a sage-green and a brownish olive-green, a pinkish lilac, a yellow (rare), and an intense black distinct from that of the black basaltes. A dark bluish-black 'solid jasper' (that is to say, coloured throughout its substance) was used in the well-known re-productions of the 'Portland Vase'. The jasper-ware of Wedgwood's own time (1780–95 has been named as the best period), and of the following twenty years or so, is distinguished by fineness and uniformity of grain, and sharpness of moulding and tooling in the reliefs, which are neither dry and chalky nor as a rule fused and glossy, though a slightly glossy variety known as 'waxen jasper' was made in small quantity at one time, about 1780.

All manner of articles were made in the jasper-ware (1) including cameos and intaglios for seals (numbering over seventeen hundred different subjects in 1779), portrait-reliefs, plaques for inlaying in furniture, beads and buttons, mounts for snuff-boxes and opera-glasses, as well as many sorts of table-ware. Wedgwood was constantly in touch with the Birmingham metalworkers, and the jasper cameos were sent there in large numbers to be mounted in their ormolu and cut-steel jewellery (2) by Boulton and Watt (previously Boulton and Fothergill), whose steam-engines Wedgwood had installed at Etruria. Large plaques were made for fireplaces in interiors such as those de-signed by the brothers Adam, with which they are in perfect harmony. Some small figures in the round were made in white jasper in the style of biscuit porcelain (3). Vases were not made until about 1781, that is to say, after the 'Wedgwood and Bentley' period; but it is said that as many as two hundred and fifty models for vases, in the stricter modern sense, besides candlesticks, ewers, flower-holders, and the like, were produced in Wedgwood's own lifetime.

The making of jasper ware, often in the old models, has continued at Wedgwood's almost without a break to the present day, but the quality of workmanship of the earlier productions has seldom been equalled.

Jasper ware was naturally much imitated by Wedgwood's rivals. In Staffordshire itself, John Turner made a greenish-toned version, in composition approaching porcelain, and William Adams a somewhat violet-toned blue in a composition like Wedgwood's own. Palmer, Neale and Wilson, and Samuel Hollins, amongst others, also made close imitations. The fashion set by Wedgwood for white reliefs on a blue ground brought many imitations of jasper ware in other materials,

(1) *Plates* 64 to 75, *Colour-Plate* C; (2) *Plate* 66A; (3) *Plate* 71A.

ranging from hard-paste porcelain down to the crudest glazed earthenware. Such imitations were made on the Continent at (amongst other places) Sèvres, Meissen, Vienna, Fürstenberg, Ansbach, Ilmenau and Doccia.

Models and modellers: It was Wedgwood's practice to adapt models and designs obtained from many sources, and in comparatively few cases is it possible to assign an artist's name to the work. Even where original models were made they were subjected to Wedgwood's own criticism and frequently altered at his suggestion, and the name of the modeller was seldom allowed to appear.

In 1769, when cameo relief-decoration was begun and the Classical style was finally adopted with the founding of Etruria, Wedgwood is known to have employed James Tassie, whose well-known casts from antique gems were used for medallions; direct access was also had for the same purpose to the Duke of Marlborough's collection. Designs for vases were taken from Sir William Hamilton's newly published catalogue of 'Etruscan' specimens, a copy of which was at once acquired by Wedgwood, also in 1769. Among the earliest relief plaques (about 1770–75) were some with 'Herculaneum figures' in cream-coloured biscuit or terra-cotta, adapted from Roman wall-paintings (1). The models used for the basaltes busts were in many cases plaster casts from the antique, and the accounts which exist for the supply of these by Grant and Hoskins, Oliver and Hoskins, Mrs. Landres, and John Flaxman, Senr., have often been mistaken for evidence of original modelling. The last-named was the father of the sculptor of the same name, who did original work for Wedgwood, though not till a later date, and many customary attributions to 'Flaxman' were erroneously based by Miss Meteyard and others on the evidence of bills for the supply of casts by the father. Some of the busts (such as the *Locke* and the *Ben Jonson*) were adapted from Rijsbrack and other contemporary sculptors.

For some time after 1787 a number of artists were employed in Rome under the direction of John Flaxman, Junr., and Henry Webber, reducing and adapting models from the antique. The well-known reproduction of the 'Barberini' (or 'Portland') vase, of Roman cameo glass (2), undertaken in 1786 and finished in 1790, is another instance of Wedgwood's practice. It is believed that not more than fifty copies of this were finished in Wedgwood's own lifetime and that not more than sixteen of these survive to-day. Many copies were made by the firm after 1845, when the original vase was broken. These copies, unlike the original issue, have the Wedgwood mark and lack the medal-

---

(1) *Plates* 48, 49; (2) *Plates* 74, 75.

lion under the foot, which is a beautiful feature of the original vase.

The portrait medallions (1) were largely adapted from medals and engraved portraits and gems, some of them undoubtedly from casts supplied by Tassie. For a series of *Popes*, medals by Dassier were copied. For some of the '*Illustrious Moderns*', an admirable series begun in 1774, wax-portraits by Matthew and Isaac Gosset and others were used; some were specially modelled by William Hackwood (among these were the *George III, Queen Charlotte* (2), *George IV as Prince of Wales, Rev. W. Willet, Josiah Wedgwood, David Garrick, Admiral Keppel, Edward Bourne*, and many others), and by John Flaxman (*Sir Frederick Herschel, Capt. James Cook, Warren Hastings, Mrs. Siddons* (3), and others). Hackwood also adapted many of the reliefs upon which the heads of 'Ancients' were based. Other contemporary modellers employed on these medallions included J. C. Lochee, Pesez and Joachim Smith (1773–74), who made portrait reliefs of both Wedgwood and Bentley and of Sir William Hamilton (4). Wedgwood invited orders for original portrait-medallions to be executed in jasper, and reliefs in wax by these and other modellers were doubtless used for the purpose. These portrait-heads are perhaps Wedgwood's most important work in jasper.

Hackwood was the principal modeller over a long period of years (1769 to 1832), working in the large busts in the early 'seventies, assembling and adapting Classical subjects (such as *The Birth of Bacchus*) (5), besides doing original work such as that already mentioned; the well-known medallion of a *Slave* (1787) was also his.

Flaxman's work for Wedgwood, which began about 1775, was evidently considerable. Apart from the portraits it is hard to identify and was probably much altered by others. A set of *Muses* (1777) (6), a relief of cupids and goats after Cipriani ('*A Sacrifice to Hymen*', 1778), a relief after the antique of *The Apotheosis of Homer* (1778) (7), groups of children ('*Blind Man's Buff*', etc., 1782) and a set of chessmen (1785) may be mentioned as probably his. The well-known 'Wine' and 'Water' vases (8) often attributed to Flaxman were probably modelled by him after the antique.

Distinct styles are shown in the sentimental-Classical reliefs of women and children, designed by Lady Templetown (9), and the bacchanalian children of Lady Diana Beauclerk (10) and Miss Crewe; but particular works by these persons cannot be identified with cer-

---

(1) *Plates* 59, 64; (2) *Plate* 59B; (3) *Plate* 64C; (4) *Plate* 64A; (5) *Plate* 73A; (6) *Plate* 65; (7) *Plate* 68; (8) compare *Plates* 60, 61; (9) *Plate* 71B, *Colour-Plate* C; (10) *Plates* 62, 65.

tainty; they probably supplied no more than preliminary sketches of the subjects customarily attributed to them.

The work of other modellers—John Voyez (1768–69), Tebo (1775), John Bacon (1777), P. Stephan, William Wood, brother of Enoch, Boot and Denby—known to have been employed, has not yet been finally identified. John Coward in 1768 supplied models for tureens and other objects in carved wood for moulding in pottery. The painter George Stubbs designed some reliefs of horses, including a *Fall of Phaethon*. The numerous modellers who worked in Rome under Flaxman and Webber included Devaere (1), Dalmazzoni, Pacetti (2), Angelini, Manzolini, 'Fratoddi', Mangianotti, and 'Cades', but their work was never signed, and being subject to adaptation at Etruria is seldom distinguishable, though further search in the archives at Barlaston may one day throw light on it.

---

(1) *Plate* 69; (2) *Plate* 72B.

3

WEDGWOOD WARE IN THE NINETEENTH CENTURY

After the death in 1810 of Wedgwood's nephew Thomas Byerley, the factory continued in charge of his son Josiah Wedgwood II until his retirement in 1841, when the latter's elder son Josiah Wedgwood III succeeded him for a short time. Francis, younger son of Josiah II, was given charge in 1844, and was followed by his son Godfrey, who became head of the firm in 1870. Francis Hamilton Wedgwood, nephew of the last-named, who had joined the firm in 1899, remained senior partner from 1905 until his death in 1930. The style of the firm has remained 'Josiah Wedgwood and Sons' from 1810 to the present day.

The fine quality reached by the wares of the first Josiah's own lifetime was maintained by his successors at least until the death of Thomas Byerley. But the later nineteenth-century Wedgwood is of little interest either to the collector or to the historian of pottery. Quietly continuing or reviving the styles (and even the patterns) of the eighteenth century and without extravagance adopting the current fashions popularised by others, the firm gradually lost its leadership of the Staffordshire industry to more adventurous, and often more vulgar, manufacturers. The period following the Napoleonic Wars was typical. Though compelled to adopt the florid gilded styles of the time, with their *parvenu* homage to Sèvres, Wedgwood's in their earthenware avoided the excesses of the Spode, Derby and Rockingham china, made to appeal to the bad taste of the 'New Rich' of the time. But the current fashions were followed. Even 'stone-china' was made for a time, and the vogue of underglaze blue and other coloured transfer-printing was shared to some extent. Though during the century no great innovation or advance was made, the firm's reputation for quality was fully maintained, especially in the blue printing (1).

Early in the nineteenth century, or even before (some say from 1792 onwards) lustre decoration began to be employed; admirable resist and incised patterns were done in 'silver' (platinum) (2), while the pink (gold) lustre and a mottled 'Moonlight' lustre were used in a

---

(1) *Plates* 82, 83; (2) *Plate* 77A.

novel way on vessels in the form of shells (1), of which specimens had earlier been borrowed from the British Museum for copying in 'pearl-ware' by the first Josiah Wedgwood himself (2). A new sort of painting in the style of the late-Chinese *famille rose* was applied with harsh effect to the black basaltes ware from about 1804 to 1810; this was called the 'chrysanthemum pattern' (3). Bone-china was made by the firm for the first time between 1812 and 1816 (4); this followed the eighteenth-century tradition, with dashing careless landscapes by John Cutts as well as simple flower-painting in the current fashion. The 'pearl ware' continued to be used for tea-services in the style of porcelain and was especially well-suited for decoration in underglaze blue.

In the second quarter of the century, the painted earthenware versions of the china were more restrained (5), and the later more naturalistic rendering of flowers more graceful and lively than most contemporary work. In the underglaze printing in blue or brown some charming Italian landscapes (6) and some magnificent floral patterns (7) were included in Wedgwood's contribution to the popular nineteenth-century style. But the barbarous 'Gothic' and other manners of the eighteen-forties, leading up to the monstrous vulgarities of the Great Exhibition of 1851, scarcely affected Wedgwood's.

The better-instructed potters of the period following the Exhibition, led by Minton's under Arnoux and closely followed by Copeland's, brought a fashion for French Renaissance styles, with biscuit figures done in 'parian' porcelain and wares with coloured glazes in Palissy style. The Staffordshire ware with coloured glazes, absurdly misnamed 'majolica', was probably inspired by the vogue of Palissy at this time, and here Wedgwood's fine green and other translucent glazes were put to good use. Many new designs for the green-glazed leaf-dishes were introduced in the second half of the nineteenth century (8), and in a singular Wedgwood style of about 1860, perhaps inspired by French ware from Rubelles, designs deeply impressed in intaglio were filled with green or brown glaze, giving a pattern in light and shade (9). The much-praised but rather facile painting of Emile Lessore (worked 1858 to 1875) belonged to the same French Renaissance fashion. The specimens here figured (10), show a rare and attractive linear manner as well as his more usual style.

A few years before 1850 Wedgwood's began an extensive revival of their eighteenth-century achievements in jasper and black basaltes;

(1) *Plate* 77B; (2) *Plate* 22B; (3) *Plate* 76; (4) *Plates* 78, 79; (5) *Plates* 80, 81; (6) *Plate* 83A; (7) *Plate* 82, 83B; (8) *Plate* 85A; (9) *Plate* 85B; (10) *Plate* 84.

new models were also made by such sculptors as Benjamin Wyon, who modelled some portrait busts of contemporaries. China began to be made again in 1878, but in general the period was not remarkable for original work. Only in some new coloured bodies did the firm maintain the tradition established by the first Josiah, of an interest in the chemistry of pottery-colours.

4

MODERN WEDGWOOD WARE

The history of Wedgwood's in the twentieth century records a continued logical progression as well as some breaks with the past, which recall the enterprise of the founder himself. In 1930 Francis Hamilton Wedgwood ('Major Frank') died after a long period as head of the firm, and in his place was appointed his nephew Josiah, second son of Josiah Clement Wedgwood, M.P. (afterwards Lord Wedgwood) and great-grandson of the Francis Wedgwood who had been senior partner in early-Victorian times. Soon after this appointment, a decision was made to leave Etruria and build new premises in the country. A site for the factory and for a model village was found at Barlaston, two miles from Stoke-on-Trent, where Barlaston Hall had for long been associated with the family. The new factory was completed and opened in 1940, though production was naturally for the time limited by the needs of a country at war.

Already under the management of Frank Wedgwood attempts had been made to break away from the conservative influences that had prevailed since the early part of the nineteenth century. About 1905, to give new life to the painted decoration, Alfred H. Powell and his wife Louise (herself a granddaughter of Emile Lessore) were engaged to design new patterns for painting and to train the painters, chiefly women, employed in the factory to execute them in free brushwork applied directly to the ware. Some of these new patterns were rich and fanciful foliate designs in the Arts-and-Crafts idiom ultimately due to William Morris; others were derived from the traditional sprig and formal patterns of the early Wedgwood and New Hall types (1). Apart from all these, which were made to be copied by the factory-hands, Alfred Powell and his wife and his wife's sister Thérèse Lessore themselves occasionally painted Wedgwood ware independently, either at the works or in their own studios, with admirable results (2). But all such work consorted a little oddly with the methods of a modern factory, which implied a different aesthetic.

It was not until more recent times that certain innovations were made, carrying the ideals and methods of the first Josiah along the

(1) *Plate* 87A; (2) *Plates* 86, 87B.

path of logical development. The production of wares in standardised shapes by casting and turning is more appropriate to a mechanised factory than the handicraft that makes and decorates each piece individually. The modern processes call for an external designer, whose approach must be governed by their requirements and possibilities and not by the standards of the craftsman. As in the most characteristic work of the first Josiah, clay-quality has in the new wares been sacrificed to precision. The engagement as designer of an architect, Keith Murray, in 1933, marked an important stage in the development of Wedgwood's ideas. Keith Murray has designed vases finished on the lathe like the Greek vases they sometimes recall, showing a sensitive precision and feeling for curve and proportion (1); while his useful wares have skilfully translated the English idiom of the earlier Staffordshire into terms appropriate to modern methods of manufacture (2). Many of the newer designs for shapes and for relief decoration done earlier in the present century, notably those of J. E. Goodwin (Art Director from 1902 to 1934), had looked back to the relief-decorated basaltes and jasper. They were done, it may be, with an eye to the American market, where Wedgwood ware in its earlier forms has continued to be greatly admired. (It indeed expresses perfectly the ideals of what is often considered the best period in the history of American taste, especially in architecture.) But Murray relied upon pure form, with a sparing use of lathe-cut bands, grooves and flutings. A manner which had in fact been introduced by the first Josiah was thus used again with an entirely modern strength and precision.

Besides introducing these new designs the Wedgwood factory continued to make table-wares in traditional forms, with an emphasis upon clean lines and efficiency in use (3). These show too a remarkable appreciation of the importance of weight and balance; there is no striving after a trivial and papery thinness, but a sensitive distribution of mass; walls and foot are substantial, and a very delicate precision is shown in the applying of handles and knobs.

Modern, too, and yet in perfect keeping with the Staffordshire tradition and the ideals of the first Josiah is the continued attention given to the chemistry of pottery and the use of coloured bodies. Much of the early Staffordshire ware of the so-called Astbury type had made use of a contrast of red-brown and white clays, in handles and spouts as well as for 'sprigged' decoration. Wedgwood in his jasper ware had exploited a similar contrast, though with layered onyx in mind rather than clay. In recent times the contrast has been used with admirable effect in precisely-made modern shapes, with newly in-

---

(1) *Plate* 91; (2) *Plate* 90; (3) *Plates* 88 89.

vented coloured bodies—such as the warm-pale-brown 'Harvest Moon',
(1) the clear light-blue 'Summer Sky', and the soft greyish 'Winter-
green', which is actually closer to the Chinese celadon than the earlier
Wedgwood body so named. The matt white 'Moonstone' was perhaps
inspired by a fine early-Chinese glaze, but it is smooth and flawless to a
degree never reached or attempted by the Chinese craftsmen. Variants
of the cream-colour were also made in the 'Champagne' body, and in
the 'Honey Buff' ('cane-colour') made for Messrs. Heal & Son, while in
china the grey and above all the 'Alpine Pink' (1936) broke new
ground. Similar work in porcelain has been done on the Continent,
where the Meissen factory was a pioneer in this department early in the
eighteenth century. Modern chemistry should make this a fruitful
field.

In decoration, too, Wedgwood's have been pioneers, producing
work which is not only charming in itself but of great significance. As
implied above, painting on modern English pottery has for long
been an anomaly on factory-made wares. Naturalistic painting of
flowers, figure-pieces, and landscapes, more or less in Sèvres style, has
remained a standard in Staffordshire, though an unattainable one, since
the skill needed has been entirely lacking. Had it been available its cost
would have been prohibitive, and it would have been in any case inap-
propriate in a modern factory. Its place has been taken by the mechan -
cally produced lithographic transfer, producing a facsimile copy of the
naturalistic flower-, figure- and other painting, and intended to deceive
the eye; or by the printing of outlines to be lifelessly filled with
colours, with the same dishonest intention and lack of aesthetic merit.

The first Josiah's use of painting was, as already stated, virtually
limited to formal flowers and foliage, generally in the form of borders
(2). Such work has hardly ever ceased to appeal to the best English and
American taste since the time of its first introduction and has latterly
enjoyed renewed popularity. New patterns have been made by
Wedgwood's in the same tradition and also in that of the simpler early
nineteenth-century porcelain of the New Hall type, with floral sprigs,
stars and formal devices. These, as designed by Alfred and Louise
Powell, Victor Skellern (who in 1934 succeeded to the post of Art Director) (3), Millicent Taplin (4), Star Wedgwood, Keith Murray (5) and
others, have been appropriate and pleasing. They are within the power
of an ordinarily skilful hand to copy, and are of course greatly superior
to the lithographic transfers.

But it may well be asked what virtue there is in brushwork of so re-

(1) *Colour-Plate* D; (2) Compare *Plates* 32 to 40; (3) *Plate* 93; (4)
Plate 92A; (5) *Plate* 92B.

D. 'HARVEST MOON' EARTHENWARE
ABOUT 1935
Victoria and Albert Museum.   See page 22

stricted a kind, when each colour may be added by a separate hand. Such work is but a step from mechanical reproduction; as painting it can convey little feeling but a sort of austere good taste and refinement. In the circumstances it might well be thought preferable to rely on the purely mechanical multiplication of a design by stencilling or better still, by the use of transfer-printing. But it must be frankly printing, in its own right so to speak, not the degraded facsimile reproduction of painting which has been usual in Staffordshire.

Transfer-printing from line-engraved and stippled copper plates had been employed by the first Josiah Wedgwood and his immediate successors, but in the course of the nineteenth century this had been degraded in the way just described. A return to the use of printing in frankly engraved work was made by Wedgwood's in 1934, when Victor Skellern produced for them his 'Forest Folk' series of engraved designs (1). These were not only very attractive in themselves but historic in marking the re-adoption of a mode of decoration that may be both aesthetically satisfying and appropriate to the factory system; it requires no great skill to apply the print to the ware, yet the process is capable of perfectly reproducing the artist's own touch and 'handwriting'.

The revival was immediately recognised as a success, and soon brought into the service of Wedgwood's one of the most gifted of English engravers, the late Eric Ravilious. Between 1936 and 1939 Ravilious produced some eight or nine designs, including an alphabet, a gardening series (2), a Coronation mug, some borders for dinner ware, a 'Boat-race bowl' (3) and a mug commemorating the removal of the factory to Barlaston. The first few of these were engraved at the factory from the designer's drawings, but the last was a lithograph drawn by Ravilious himself for direct application to the ware. His work showed a characteristic grave simplicity, quiet humour, and above all a most imaginative use of the textures produced by the graver. His death in the War was a very great loss.

The modelling of pottery figures was never greatly favoured at Etruria. For Wedgwood himself they were too closely associated with the frivolity of Rococo porcelain. Only when the introduction of biscuit facilitated the imitation of Classical marble and stone did he make a few figures in the round. (The glazed and coloured earthenware figures sometimes bearing his mark were made for him by other potters: see Marks, p. 28 below.) His successors, though occasionally employing contemporary sculptors to make new models for jasper ware, broke no new ground in this direction until quite recent times.

(1) *Plate* 94A; (2) *Plate* 95; (3) *Plate* 94B.

In 1926 the sculptor John Skeaping was employed to model some figures and reliefs of animals for reproduction in cream-coloured and 'Moonstone' ware, and more recently Arnold Machin has modelled a *Bull* (1) and a *Wedding Group* (2), amongst others, which at first glance appear to belong to the tradition of the early-Victorian Staffordshire figures, but are actually modelled with a rare subtlety. None of these, or the more serious work also done by the same modeller, has shown its quality in the result, for lack of a material more distinguished than the ordinary ware used for table-services and the like. The forms have been generalised and have lost distinctness in the process of multiplying the models. Only relatively insignificant trade figures are possible in such a medium, however well they may be modelled. The superb modern figures of other factories—such as those made by Paul Scheurich at Meissen and Berlin, by Arno Malinowski and Jais Nielsen at Copenhagen and by Georges Serre at Sèvres—have had the advantage of an exquisitely fine porcelain or a rugged and masculine stoneware in the early-Chinese manner. Such a material alone can embody adequately a distinguished plastic conception. Now the first Josiah Wedgwood spent great efforts in research after a ware distinguished enough for his imitations of engraved gems, and eventually found it in the jasper ware in which so much of his finest work was done. This as I contend was but a by-path, aside from the main course of English ceramic evolution, though the delight it gave and still gives, made it valuable. A comparable research by Wedgwoods in the twentieth century, inspired by the early Chinese as the other was inspired by Classical art, might also produce a material worthy of their modeller's genius. This again would be a complementary activity, producing objects of art delightful for their own sake but standing apart from the finely designed and beautifully made table-wares on which the fame of Wedgwood must always rest.

---

(1) *Plate* 96B; (2) *Plate* 96A.

MARKS

All impressed

WEDGWOOD
& BENTLEY
(1)

W & B
(2)

Wedgwood
& Bentley
(3)

(4)

WEDGWOOD
(5)

Wedgwood
(6)

WDP
WEDGWOOD
W
(7)

The pre-Etruria productions were very seldom if ever marked; authenticated examples of the wares sometimes alleged to have been marked 'Wedgwood' in irregular lettering cannot be cited.

(1) to (4) are marks of the Wedgwood and Bentley period (1768–80). A circular mark without 'Etruria' is also stated to occur but is very rare.

(5) and (6) are later marks (1771 onwards on useful wares; 1780 onwards on all classes of ware). The word 'WEDGWOOD' printed in red or (more rarely) in blue or gold occurs on china made between 1812 and 1816.

(7) Modern mark, always in capitals. The three letters side by side occur in marks dating from 1860 to 1928; the third of these letters is a year-cipher in a series beginning with O for 1860 and following the alphabet; thus the specimen given indicates the year 1861. This series was continued, A following Z and so on in fresh cycles, until 1929, when a four-numeral mark was introduced, of which the last two numerals—'29', etc.—stand for the year. The letters of the nineteenth century and modern marks are placed somewhat more regularly than in the old. The numerals in the marks on the eighteenth-century cameos, etc. are sometimes catalogue-numbers or mould-numbers, or (in the case of useful wares) size-numbers. The initials which sometimes appear are often supposed to be workmen's marks, but may perhaps be signs for different pastes. Wedgwood was in general opposed to the use of any sort of signatures by workmen, and the interpre-

tation of, for example, 'K' for Keeling and 'H' for Hackwood, is conjectural only and on general grounds improbable. The rare signatures of Hackwood occur on the face of the piece. The random tool-marks (stars, claws or commas, etc.) impressed, often in pairs with numerals and letters, are workmen's marks and usually indicate a date in the early part of the nineteenth century, as does a mark with a letter forming part of the same stamp as the 'WEDGWOOD'.

The word 'PEARL' was added at first on the white pearl-ware made from 1780 onwards.

A very rare mark 'Josiah Wedgwood Feb 2 1805' is supposed to have been used on the occasion of the testing of a new pyrometer invented by Josiah Wedgwood II.

The word 'Etruria' is said to have been added for a short time about 1840, and again about 1890 when the mark 'Josiah Wedgwood & Sons Etruria' is said to have been in use. The word 'England' began to be used in 1891 on wares for the American market to comply with the McKinley Act of that year, which required the mark on imported wares to state the country of origin. A representation of the Portland Vase began to be used as a printed mark on china from 1878.

The 'Wedgwood' mark, it should be noted, occasionally appears on eighteenth-century Staffordshire wares of types not known to have been made by Josiah Wedgwood. Some of these pieces were apparently made by other potters on his behalf to complete orders from abroad. There is documentary evidence from the Wood family side to show that Ralph Wood occasionally supplied Wedgwood with pottery figures (such as the big *Virgin and Child* and the bust known as *Sadness*), and it is likely that Pratt supplied reliefs in the same way. And it is also certain that the mark was used fraudulently by other potters, both in England and abroad (where the 'D' and 'G' were apt to get reversed); the Hubertusburg factory in Saxony in the eighteenth century and a Dutch potter in the nineteenth century, among others, are known to have used the mark. Other members of the Wedgwood family were also potters and sometimes honestly used the name as a mark.

The following should be noted:

'WEDGWOOD & SONS' is said to occur on Etruria wares dating from about 1790; it is very rare.

'WEDGWOOD & Co' is the mark of Ralph Wedgwood of the Hill Works, Burslem and Ferrybridge in Yorkshire (eighteenth century), a kinsman of Josiah's. It is also the style of a modern Staffordshire firm at Tunstall.

'WEDGEWOOD' is the mark of W. Smith & Co. of Stockton-on-Tees (1826 onwards), against whom in 1848 an injunction was granted at the instance of Josiah Wedgwood & Sons, on account of the misuse of their name.

According to Jewitt, William Baddeley, of Eastwood near Hanley (about 1802–22), used the place-name with the first syllable blurred, with the intention that it should be mistaken for 'Wedgwood', on wares in Wedgwood style. The mark on a specimen in the Schreiber Collection is, however, perfectly distinct.

BIBLIOGRAPHY
The more important works are indicated by an asterisk

Josiah Wedgwood's catalogues of his productions, 1775 onwards.
Josiah Wedgwood's correspondence (*Wedgwood's letters to Bentley*, 1762–80, two volumes, edited by K. E. Farrer, London, 1903; *Correspondence of Josiah Wedgwood*, edited by K. E. Farrer, London, 1906).
Llewellynn Jewitt, *The Wedgwoods, being a life of Josiah Wedgwood*, London, 1865.
Eliza Meteyard, *Life of Josiah Wedgwood.* London, 1865–66.
Eliza Meteyard, *Handbook of Wedgwood Ware.* London, 1875.
*C. T. Gatty, *Liverpool Art Club: Catalogue of a loan collection of the works of Josiah Wedgwood.* Liverpool, 1879.
F. Rathbone (Birmingham Museum and Art Gallery), *Old Wedgwood: Handbook to the Collection formed by Richard and George Tangye.* Birmingham, 1885.
F. Rathbone, *Old Wedgwood.* London, 1893.
*A. H. Church, *Josiah Wedgwood, Master Potter.* London, 1903.
R. L. Hobson, *Catalogue of English Pottery in the British Museum.* London, 1903.
William Burton, *A History and Description of English Earthenware and Stoneware.* London, 1904.
*F. Rathbone, *Catalogue of the Wedgwood Museum, Etruria.* Stoke-on-Trent, 1909.
*William Burton, *Josiah Wedgwood and his pottery.* London, 1922.
Bernar d Rackham and Herbert Read, *English Pottery.* London, 1924.
*HarryBarnard, *Chats on Wedgwood ware.* London, 1924.
R. L. Hobson, *Chinese Porcelain and Wedgwood Pottery* (catalogue of the collection in the Lady Lever Art Gallery, Port Sunlight). London, 1928.
Jean Gorely and Mary Wadsworth (Harvard University, Fogg Museum of Art), *Catalogue of an Exhibition of Old Wedgwood from the Bequest of Grenville Lindall Winthrop.* Cambridge (Mass.), 1944.

THE WEDGWOOD FAMILY OF POTTERS

showing dates of partnership in the firm of Josiah Wedgwood & Sons, Ltd. The names of senior partners and Managing Directors are shown in capitals.

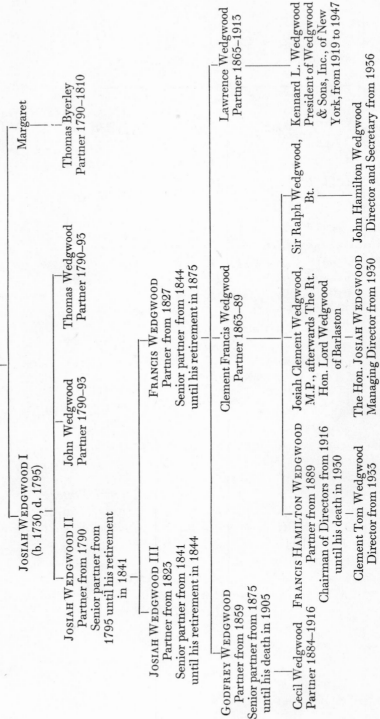

Thomas Wedgwood

Margaret — Thomas Byerley
Partner 1790–1810

JOSIAH WEDGWOOD I
(b. 1730, d. 1795)

JOSIAH WEDGWOOD II
Partner from 1790
Senior partner from
1795 until his retirement
in 1841

John Wedgwood
Partner 1790–93

Thomas Wedgwood
Partner 1790–93

JOSIAH WEDGWOOD III
Partner from 1823
Senior partner from 1841
until his retirement in 1844

FRANCIS WEDGWOOD
Partner from 1827
Senior partner from 1844
until his retirement in 1875

GODFREY WEDGWOOD
Partner from 1859
Senior partner from 1875
until his death in 1905

Clement Francis Wedgwood
Partner 1863–89

Lawrence Wedgwood
Partner 1865–1913

Cecil Wedgwood
Partner 1884–1916

FRANCIS HAMILTON WEDGWOOD
Partner from 1889
Chairman of Directors from 1916
until his death in 1930

Josiah Clement Wedgwood,
M.P., afterwards The Rt.
Hon. Lord Wedgwood
of Barlaston

Sir Ralph Wedgwood,
Bt.

Kennard L. Wedgwood
President of Wedgwood
& Sons, Inc., of New
York, from 1919 to 1947

Clement Tom Wedgwood
Director from 1933

The Hon. JOSIAH WEDGWOOD
Managing Director from 1930

John Hamilton Wedgwood
Director and Secretary from 1936

INDEX

INDEX

INDEX

1. TEAPOT, EARTHENWARE WITH GREEN AND YELLOW GLAZES
ABOUT 1760–65
Burslem, Wedgwood Institute
See page 9

2. TEAPOT, EARTHENWARE WITH *chinoiseries* IN RELIEF, GREEN
AND YELLOW GLAZES. ABOUT 1760–65
Victoria and Albert Museum
See pages, 9 ,10

3. TEAPOT, EARTHENWARE WITH LANDSCAPES IN RELIEF,
GREEN AND YELLOW GLAZES. ABOUT 1760–65
Schreiber Collection
See page 9

4. TUREEN, EARTHENWARE WITH GREEN, YELLOW AND PURPLE-
BROWN GLAZES. ABOUT 1760–65
Fitzwilliam Museum (Glaisher Collection) Cambridge
See pages 9, 10

5. BOWL, EARTHENWARE WITH PURPLE, BLUE AND GREEN
GLAZES. ABOUT 1760–65
Fitzwilliam Museum (Glaisher Collection) Cambridge
See pages 9, 10

6A. TEAPOT, EARTHENWARE WITH YELLOWISH GLAZE STRIPED
WITH GREENISH GREY. ABOUT 1760–65
T. Murray Ragg
See page 9

6B. TEAPOT, EARTHENWARE WITH YELLOWISH GLAZE STRIPED
WITH GREEN. ABOUT 1760–65
J. L. Dixon
See page 9

7A. BOTTLE, SALT-GLAZED STONEWARE. ABOUT 1760
Schreiber Collection
See page 9
7B. BOWL, CREAM EARTHENWARE WITH YELLOWISH GLAZE
TOUCHED WITH GREEN AND PURPLE. ABOUT 1760
Victoria and Albert Museum
See pages 9, 10

8. TEAPOT, EARTHENWARE, WITH GREEN AND YELLOW GLAZES
ABOUT 1760–65
Schreiber Collection
See page 9

9. TEAPOT, EARTHENWARE, WITH GREEN AND YELLOW GLAZES
ABOUT 1760–65
Schreiber Collection
See page 9

10. TEAPOT, SALT-GLAZED STONEWARE, ENAMELLED IN COLOURS
PERHAPS AT LEEDS
ABOUT 1765
Schreiber Collection
See pages 9, 10

11. TEAPOT, EARTHENWARE, WITH GREEN GLAZE AND GILDING
ABOUT 1760–65
Victoria and Albert Museum
See page 9

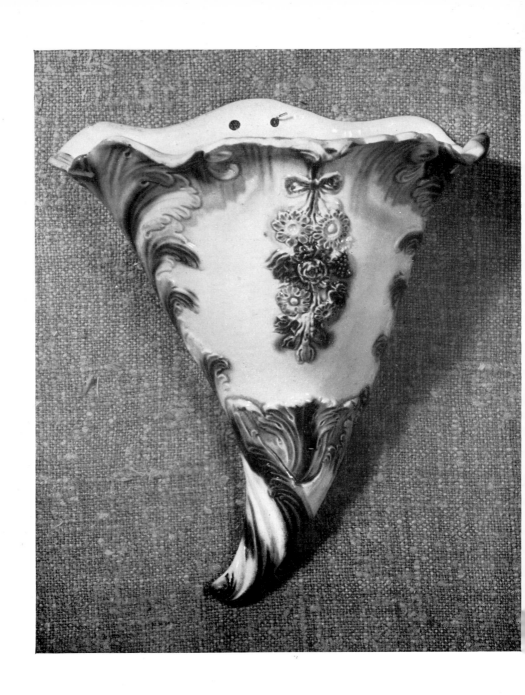

12. FLOWER-HOLDER, EARTHENWARE, WITH GREEN
AND PURPLE-BROWN GLAZES
ABOUT 1760–65
J. L. Dixon
See pages, 9, 10

13. FLOWER-HOLDER, SALT-GLAZED STONEWARE
ABOUT 1760–65
Schreiber Collection
See pages 9, 10

14. TEAPOT, UNGLAZED RED STONEWARE, WITH ENGINE-TURNED
DECORATION. IMITATION CHINESE MARK. ABOUT 1765
Mrs. Cecil Ward
See page 14

15A. CREAM-POT, UNGLAZED RED STONEWARE
ABOUT 1765–75
Victoria and Albert Museum
See page 14
15B. TEAPOT, UNGLAZED RED STONEWARE. MARK, WEDGWOOD
LATE 18TH OR EARLY 19TH CENTURY
Victoria and Albert Museum
See page 14

16. TEAPOT, CREAM-COLOURED WARE, ENAMELLED IN COLOURS,
CHIEFLY RED AND BLACK, PERHAPS AT LEEDS
ABOUT 1765–75
Victoria and Albert Museum
See pages 11, 12

17. TEAPOT, CREAM-COLOURED WARE, ENAMELLED IN COLOURS,
CHIEFLY RED AND BLACK, PERHAPS AT LEEDS
ABOUT 1765–75
T. Murray Ragg
See pages 11, 12

18. JUG, CREAM-COLOURED WARE
ABOUT 1765–75
Victoria and Albert Museum
See page 11

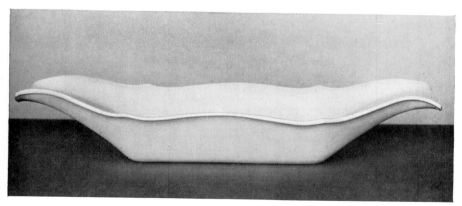

19A. JAM-POT, CREAM-COLOURED WARE. MARK, 'WEDGWOOD'
LATE EIGHTEENTH CENTURY
19B. ASPARAGUS-DISH, CREAM-COLOURED WARE. MARK, 'WEDGWOOD'
LATE EIGHTEENTH OR EARLY NINETEENTH CENTURY
Victoria and Albert Museum
See page 11

20. CHESTNUT-BASKET, CREAM-COLOURED WARE. MARK, 'WEDGWOOD'
LATE EIGHTEENTH CENTURY
Victoria and Albert Museum
See page 11

21. FOOD-WARMER, CREAM-COLOURED WARE. MARK, 'WEDGWOOD'
LATE EIGHTEENTH OR EARLY NINETEENTH CENTURY
J. L. Dixon.
See page 11

22A. TOY WATERING-CAN(?), CREAM-COLOURED WARE
LATE EIGHTEENTH CENTURY
Victoria and Albert Museum
See page 11
22B. TUREEN, 'PEARL' WARE. MARK, 'WEDGWOOD'
AND 'B'
LATE EIGHTEENTH OR EARLY NINETEENTH CENTURY
Victoria and Albert Museum
See pages 11, 20

23A. SAUCE-BOAT, CREAM-COLOURED WARE
ABOUT 1765–75
Victoria and Albert Museum
See page 11
23B. CRUET, CREAM-COLOURED WARE. MARK, 'WEDGWOOD'
LATE EIGHTEENTH CENTURY
Victoria and Albert Museum
See page 11

24. JUG, CREAM-COLOURED WARE, PRINTED IN PURPLE
MARK, 'WEDGWOOD' AND 'I'
ABOUT 1770
Schreiber Collection
See pages 11, 12

25A. DISH, CREAM-COLOURED WARE, PAINTED IN PURPLE
MARK, 'WEDGWOOD'
ABOUT 1770
Victoria and Albert Museum
See page 11

25A. DISH, CREAM-COLOURED WARE, PRINTED IN BLACK AND
PAINTED OVER IN GREEN. MARK, 'WEDGWOOD'
ABOUT 1770
Victoria and Albert Museum
See pages, 11, 12

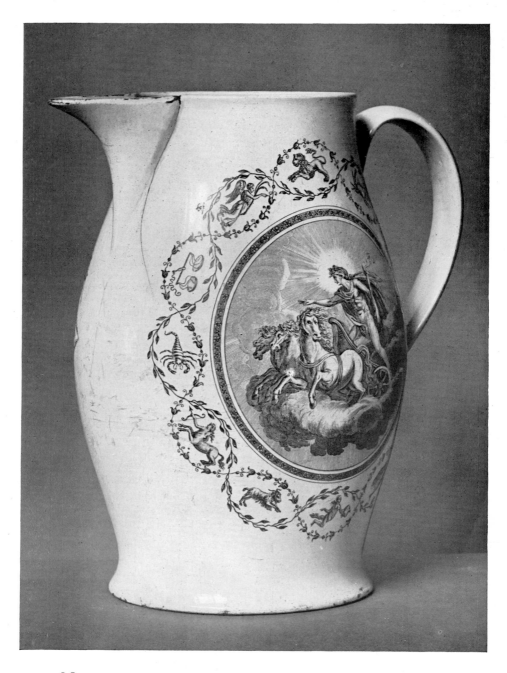

26. JUG, CREAM-COLOURED WARE, PRINTED IN BLACK,
PROBABLY AT LIVERPOOL
ABOUT 1775
Liverpool Public Museum
See pages 11, 12

27. JUG, CREAM-COLOURED WARE, PRINTED IN BLACK,
PROBABLY AT LIVERPOOL, THE INITIALS PAINTED
ABOUT 1775
Schreiber Collection
See pages 11, 12

28. TEAPOT, CREAM-COLOURED WARE, PRINTED IN RED,
PROBABLY AT LIVERPOOL. MARK, 'WEDGWOOD'
ABOUT 1770
Victoria and Albert Museum
See pages 11, 12

29. PLATE, CREAM-COLOURED WARE, PRINTED IN RED AND
PAINTED IN GREEN, PROBABLY AT LIVERPOOL
MARK, 'WEDGWOOD'
ABOUT 1775
Schreiber Collection
See pages 11, 12

50. DISH, CREAM-COLOURED WARE, PRINTED IN BLACK,
PROBABLY AT LIVERPOOL. MARK, 'WEDGWOOD'
ABOUT 1780
Schreiber Collection
See pages 11, 12

31. DISH, CREAM-COLOURED WARE, PRINTED IN BLACK,
PROBABLY AT LIVERPOOL. MARK, 'WEDGWOOD'
ABOUT 1780
Schreiber Collection
See pages 11, 12

32A. PLATE, CREAM-COLOURED WARE, PAINTED IN BROWN AND BLUE
MARK, 'WEDGWOOD'
LATE EIGHTEENTH CENTURY
Victoria and Albert Museum. See pages 11, 12
32B. SUPPER-DISHES, CREAM-COLOURED WARE, PAINTED IN
BROWN AND YELLOW. MARK, 'WEDGWOOD'
LATE EIGHTEENTH CENTURY
Victoria and Albert Museum. See pages 11, 12

33A. PLATE, CREAM-COLOURED WARE, PAINTED IN BROWN
AND GREEN. MARK, 'WEDGWOOD' AND A STAR
LATE EIGHTEENTH CENTURY
Victoria and Albert Museum
See pages 11, 12
33B. TUREEN, CREAM-COLOURED WARE, PAINTED IN BROWN
AND GREY, WITH A DUTCH INSCRIPTION. DATED 1804
MARK, 'WEDGWOOD'
Schreiber Collection
See pages 11, 12

34. DISH, CREAM-COLOURED WARE, PAINTED IN PINK AND GREEN
MARK, 'WEDGWOOD' AND 'P'
ABOUT 1780
Reproduced by gracious permission of His Majesty The King
See pages 11, 12

35. JUG, CREAM-COLOURED WARE, PAINTED IN COLOURS
MARK, 'WEDGWOOD', ALSO '6'. ABOUT 1780
Victoria and Albert Museum
See pages 11, 12

36. TUREEN, CREAM-COLOURED WARE, PAINTED IN BLACK
MARK, 'WEDGWOOD'
LATE EIGHTEENTH CENTURY
Victoria and Albert Museum
See pages 11, 12

37A. CUP, CREAM-COLOURED WARE, PAINTED IN
BROWN. MARK, 'WEDGWOOD'
LATE EIGHTEENTH CENTURY
Victoria and Albert Museum
See pages 11, 12
37B. BUTTER-DISH, CREAM-COLOURED WARE,
PAINTED IN COLOURS. MARK, 'WEDGWOOD'
ABOUT 1780
Mrs. Drummond
See pages 11, 12

38. DISH, CREAM-COLOURED WARE, PAINTED IN GREEN, BLUE
AND BLACK. MARK, 'WEDGWOOD'
ABOUT 1780
Victoria and Albert Museum
See pages 11, 12

39A. PLATE, CREAM-COLOURED WARE, PAINTED IN RED AND
BLACK. MARK, 'WEDGWOOD' AND A TOOL MARK
LATE EIGHTEENTH OR EARLY NINETEENTH CENTURY
Victoria and Albert Museum
See pages 11, 12
39B. DISH, CREAM-COLOURED WARE, PAINTED IN COLOURS
MARK, 'WEDGWOOD' AND '3'
LATE EIGHTEENTH CENTURY
Victoria and Albert Museum
See pages 11, 12

40. CUP, COVER AND SAUCER, CREAM-COLOURED WARE, PAINTED
IN RED AND BROWN. MARK, 'WEDGWOOD' AND 'C'
LATE EIGHTEENTH CENTURY
Victoria and Albert Museum
See pages 11, 12
40B. BOWL AND STAND, CREAM-COLOURED WARE, PAINTED IN
BLACK AND RED. MARK, 'WEDGWOOD' 'AND 'C'
LATE EIGHTEENTH CENTURY
Victoria and Albert Museum
See pages 11, 12

41. PLATE FROM THE IMPERIAL RUSSIAN SERVICE, CREAM-
COLOURED WARE, PAINTED IN PURPLISH BLACK, THE CREST
IN GREEN. MARK, '207' IN BLACK
MADE IN 1773–74
Victoria and Albert Museum
See pages 11, 12

42. VASE, CREAM-COLOURED WARE, WITH DECORATION IN
BROWN SLIP, ENGINE-TURNED
LATE EIGHTEENTH CENTURY
Burslem, Wedgwood Institute
See page 13

43. VASE, CREAM-COLOURED WARE, WITH MOTTLED DECORATION
IN DULL BLUE. MARK, 'WEDGWOOD & BENTLEY ETRURIA'
ON A CIRCULAR BAND
ABOUT 1770
Victoria and Albert Museum
See page 13

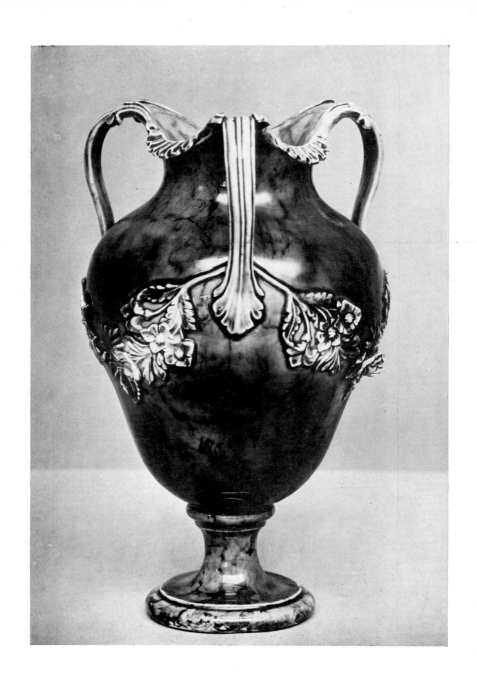

44. VASE, CREAM-COLOURED WARE WITH COLOURED GLAZES
MARK, 'WEDGWOOD & BENTLEY'
ABOUT 1770
Wedgwood Museum
See page 13

45. VASE, WITH MARBLED GLAZE. MARK, 'WEDGWOOD
& BENTLEY'. ABOUT 1770
Victoria and Albert Museum
See page 13

46. EWER, AGATE WARE. MARK, 'WEDGWOOD &
BENTLEY ETRURIA' ON A CIRCULAR BAND
ABOUT 1770
Victoria and Albert Museum
See page 13

47. VASE, AGATE WARE. MARK, 'WEDGWOOD & BENTLEY
ETRURIA' ON A CIRCULAR BAND. ABOUT 1770
Burslem, Wedgwood Institute
See page 13

48. PANEL, BISCUIT-COLOURED WARE
ABOUT 1770–75
Victoria and Albert Museum
See page 16

49. PANEL, BISCUIT-COLOURED WARE
ABOUT 1770-75
Victoria and Albert Museum
See page 16

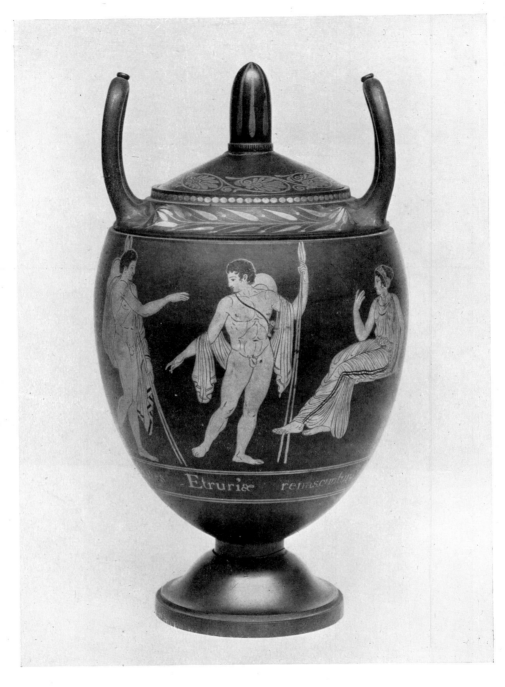

50. VASE, BLACK-BASALTES WARE, WITH ENAMEL PAINTING
THE FIRST VASE MADE AT ETRURIA (1769)
Wedgwood Museum
See page 13

51. PANELS, BLACK-BASALTES WARE, WITH ENAMEL PAINTING
ABOUT 1770–75
Mrs. David Davis
See page 13

52. VASE, BLACK-BASALTES WARE, WITH ENAMEL PAINTING
MARK, 'WEDGWOOD'
LATE EIGHTEENTH CENTURY
Victoria and Albert Museum
See page 13

53A. TEAPOT, BLACK-BASALTES WARE, WITH ENAMEL PAINTING
MARK, 'WEDGWOOD & BENTLEY'
ABOUT 1770–80
Victoria and Albert Museum
See page 13
53B. CUP AND SAUCER, BLACK-BASALTES WARE, WITH ENAMEL
PAINTING. MARK, 'WEDGWOOD'
ABOUT 1770–80 OR LATER
Victoria and Albert Museum
See page 13

54. LIBRARY BUST OF SENECA, BLACK-BASALTES WARE
MARK, 'WEDGWOOD'
ABOUT 1785
Victoria and Albert Museum
See page 13

55. FIGURE OF VOLTAIRE, BLACK-BASALTES WARE
ABOUT 1777
Victoria and Albert Museum
See page 13

56. TEAPOT, BLACK-BASALTES WARE, THE RELIEFS ('THE
DANCING HOURS') FROM A MODEL ORIGINALLY MADE BY
JOHN FLAXMAN IN 1775 BUT ALTERED BY THE ADDITION OF
DRAPERIES BY WILLIAM HACKWOOD IN 1802. MARK, 'WEDGWOOD'
EARLY NINETEENTH CENTURY
Victoria and Albert Museum
See page 14

57. VASE, BLACK-BASALTES WARE. MARK, 'WEDGWOOD'
ABOUT 1785
Victoria and Albert Museum
See pages 13, 14

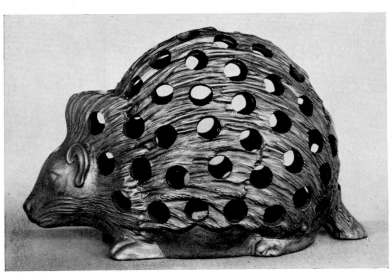

58A. PANEL. B. BRAZIER. BLACK-BASALTES WARE
ABOUT 1775
Victoria and Albert Museum
See page 14

59A. CAMEOS AND AN INTAGLIO, BLACK-BASALTES WARE
ABOUT 1770–80
59B. MEDALLION PORTRAIT-RELIEFS OF BENJAMIN FRANKLIN,
QUEEN CHARLOTTE (FROM A MODEL BY WILLIAM HACKWOOD,
1777), JAN DE WITT, AND VOLTAIRE; BLACK-BASALTES WARE
SOME MARKED 'WEDGWOOD & BENTLEY' OR 'WEDGWOOD'
ABOUT 1775–95
Victoria and Albert Museum
See pages 14, 17

60. VASE, BLACK-BASALTES WARE. MARK, 'WEDGWOOD'
ABOUT 1775 OR LATER
Burslem, Wedgwood Institute
See pages 14, 17

61. VASE, BLACK-BASALTES WARE. MARK, 'WEDGWOOD'
ABOUT 1775 OR LATER
Victoria and Albert Museum
See pages 14, 17

62. TEAPOT, CANE-COLOURED STONEWARE WITH ENAMEL PAINTING
MARK, 'WEDGWOOD' AND '2'
LATE EIGHTEENTH OR EARLY NINETEENTH CENTURY
Victoria and Albert Museum
See pages 14, 17

63. VASE, BISCUIT-COLOURED STONEWARE WITH DARK-BROWN
RELIEFS. MARK, 'WEDGWOOD'
EARLY NINETEENTH CENTURY
Victoria and Albert Museum
See page 14

64. MEDALLION PORTRAIT-RELIEFS IN BISCUIT-COLOURED WARE
AND BLUE JASPER-WARE OF SIR WILLIAM HAMILTON (FROM A
MODEL BY JOACHIM SMITH, 1773), WARREN HASTINGS AND
MRS. SIDDONS (FROM MODELS BY JOHN FLAXMAN, 1784) AND
THOMAS BENTLEY (FROM A MODEL BY JOACHIM SMITH, 1773)
SOME MARKED 'WEDGWOOD & BENTLEY' OR 'WEDGWOOD'
ABOUT 1773–85

Mrs. David Davis and *Victoria and Albert Museum*
See pages 15, 17

65. RELIEFS IN BLUE AND BLACK JASPER-WARE, SOME
MARKED 'WEDGWOOD'
ABOUT 1770–90
Victoria and Albert Museum
See pages 15, 17

66A. MEDALLION RELIEF IN JASPER-WARE, MOUNTED IN CUT STEEL
ABOUT 1785
Schreiber Collection
See page 15
66B. IVORY BOX, WITH BLUE JASPER-WARE RELIEFS
ABOUT 1775
Nottingham Castle Museum
See page 15

67. CANDELABRUM WITH JASPER-WARE RELIEFS,
MOUNTED WITH CUT GLASS AND ORMOLU
LATE EIGHTEENTH CENTURY
Victoria and Albert Museum
See page 15

68. VASE, BLUE JASPER-WARE: 'THE APOTHEOSIS OF HOMER'
THE RELIEFS AFTER A MODEL BY JOHN FLAXMAN
MARK, 'WEDGWOOD'
ABOUT 1789
Nottingham Museum and Art Gallery
See pages 15, 17

69. VASE, BLACK JASPER-WARE: 'THE TRIUMPH OF BACCHUS',
THE RELIEFS AFTER A MODEL MADE IN ROME BY JOHN
DEVAERE FROM THE 'BORGHESE VASE' NOW IN
THE LOUVRE. MARK, 'WEDGWOOD'
ABOUT 1785
Nottingham Museum and Art Gallery
See pages 15, 18

70A. JAR, BLUE JASPER-WARE. MARK, 'WEDGWOOD'
LATE EIGHTEENTH CENTURY
Mrs. David Davis
See page 15
70B. BOWL, BLUE JASPER-WARE. MARK, 'WEDGWOOD'
LATE EIGHTEENTH CENTURY
Victoria and Albert Museum
See page 15

71A. BUST, WHITE JASPER-WARE
LATE EIGHTEENTH CENTURY
Schreiber Collection
See page 15
71B. TEAPOT, GREEN JASPER-WARE. MARK, 'WEDGWOOD'
LATE EIGHTEENTH CENTURY
Schreiber Collection
See pages 15, 17

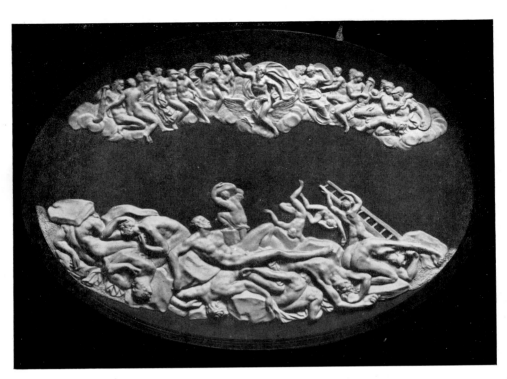

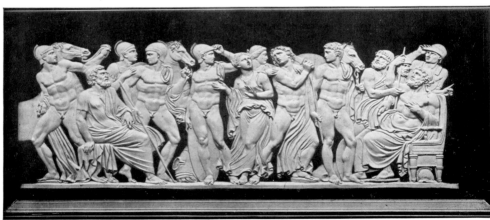

72A. RELIEF: 'FALL OF TITANS', BLUE JASPER-WARE
LATE EIGHTEENTH CENTURY
Mrs. David Davis
See page 15
72B. RELIEF: FROM A MODEL MADE IN ROME IN 1787–8 BY
PACETTI, FROM THE ROMAN SARCOPHAGUS IN WHICH THE
'PORTLAND VASE' WAS FOUND. BLUE JASPER-WARE
LATE EIGHTEENTH CENTURY
J. A. Tulk
See pages 15, 18

73A. RELIEF: BACCHUS AND MERCURY, BLUE JASPER-WARE,
AFTER A MODEL BY WILLIAM HACKWOOD
LATE EIGHTEENTH CENTURY
Mrs. David Davis
See pages 15, 17
73B. RELIEF: APOLLO AND THE MUSES, BLUE JASPER-WARE.
LATE EIGHTEENTH CENTURY
Mrs. David Davis
See page 15

74. WEDGWOOD'S COPY OF 'THE PORTLAND VASE', BLUE
JASPER-WARE. FORMERLY THE PROPERTY OF CHARLES DARWIN,
THE NATURALIST (GRANDSON OF JOSIAH WEDGWOOD), WHOSE
FATHER BOUGHT IT FROM THE POTTER IN 1793
ABOUT 1786–90
Victoria and Albert Museum
See page 16

75. BASE OF 'THE PORTLAND VASE'
See pages 15, 16

76. COFFEE-POT, BLACK-BASALTES WARE, WITH ENAMEL PAINTING
MARK, 'WEDGWOOD'
ABOUT 1804–10
Victoria and Albert Museum
See page 20

77A. CANDLESTICK, WHITE EARTHENWARE WITH DECORATION
IN PLATINUM ('SILVER') LUSTRE. MARK, 'WEDGWOOD' AND 'J'
EARLY NINETEENTH CENTURY
Victoria and Albert Museum
See page 19
77B. SHELL-VASE, WHITE EARTHENWARE COVERED WITH
PINK LUSTRE. MARK, 'WEDGWOOD'
EARLY NINETEENTH CENTURY
Victoria and Albert Museum
See page 20

78. TABLE-WARES, BONE-CHINA, PAINTED BY JOHN CUTTS
MARK, 'WEDGWOOD', PRINTED IN RED
ABOUT 1812–16
Victoria and Albert Museum
See page 20

79. TABLE-WARES, BONE-CHINA. MARK, 'WEDGWOOD',
PRINTED IN RED
ABOUT 1812–16
Victoria and Albert Museum
See page 20

80A. MUG, PAINTED IN COLOURS, GREEN GROUND
MARK, 'WEDGWOOD'
ABOUT 1840
Victoria and Albert Museum
See page 20

80B. PLATE, PAINTED IN COLOURS, GREY-GREEN GROUND
MARK, 'WEDGWOOD'
ABOUT 1835
Victoria and Albert Museum
See page 20

81. PLATE, PAINTED IN COLOURS, PALE LAVENDER GROUND
MARK, 'WEDGWOOD'
ABOUT 1840
Victoria and Albert Museum
See page 20

82. STRAINER, WHITE EARTHENWARE, PRINTED IN BLUE
MARK, 'WEDGWOOD' AND '20'
MIDDLE OF NINETEENTH CENTURY
Victoria and Albert Museum
See pages 19, 20

83A. CUP AND SAUCER, WHITE EARTHENWARE PRINTED IN
BROWN. MARK, 'WEDGWOOD'
ABOUT 1835
Victoria and Albert Museum
See pages 19, 20

83B. DISH, WHITE EARTHENWARE, PRINTED IN BLUE
MARK, 'WEDGWOOD'
FIRST HALF OF NINETEENTH CENTURY
Victoria and Albert Museum
See pages 19, 20

84A. VASE, CREAM-COLOURED WARE, PAINTED AND SIGNED BY
EMILE LESSORE. MARK, 'WEDGWOOD' AND 'WUQ'
DATED 1862
Victoria and Albert Museum
See page 20

84B. TRAY, CREAM-COLOURED WARE, PAINTED AND SIGNED BY
EMILE LESSORE. MARK, 'WEDGWOOD' AND 'HTU'
DATED 1866
Victoria and Albert Museum
See page 20

85A. DISH, GREEN-GLAZED EARTHENWARE
MARK, 'WEDGWOOD' AND '1'
ABOUT 1860
Victoria and Albert Museum
See pages 10, 20
85B. DISH, WITH PANEL IN RELIEF COVERED WITH GREEN GLAZE
MARK, 'WEDGWOOD' AND 'COS'
DATED 1864
Victoria and Albert Museum
See page 20

86. VASE, DESIGNED AND PAINTED BY ALFRED H. POWELL
ONE OF A SET MADE FOR SIR HUGH BELL'S HOUSE AT
ROUNTON, YORKSHIRE
ABOUT 1920
Bethnal Green Museum
See page 22

87A. MUG, DESIGNED AND PAINTED BY ALFRED H. AND
LOUISE POWELL
ABOUT 1920
Bethnal Green Museum
See page 22
87B. PLATE, PAINTED BY THÉRÈSE LESSORE
ABOUT 1925
Bethnal Green Museum
See page 22

88. VASE, CANE-COLOURED ('HONEYBUFF') WARE
ABOUT 1920
Messrs. Heal & Son, Ltd
See page 23

89A. TABLE-WARES IN BONE-CHINA
ABOUT 1940
See page 23
89B. TABLE-WARES IN CREAM-COLOURED WARE
ABOUT 1935
See page 23

90. MUGS AND JUGS DESIGNED BY KEITH MURRAY
ABOUT 1935
See page 23

91. VASE AND BOWL DESIGNED BY KEITH MURRAY
ABOUT 1935
See page 23

92. TABLE-WARES IN BONE-CHINA WITH PAINTED DECORATION
DESIGNED BY (A) MILLICENT TAPLIN AND (B) KEITH MURRAY
ABOUT 1935
See page 24

93. TABLE-WARES IN BONE-CHINA WITH PAINTED DECORATION
DESIGNED BY VICTOR SKELLERN
ABOUT 1935
See page 24

94A. PLATE, CREAM-COLOURED WARE WITH PRINTED DECORATION
DESIGNED BY VICTOR SKELLERN
ABOUT 1934
See page 25

94B. BOWL, CREAM-COLOURED WARE WITH PRINTED DECORATION
DESIGNED BY ERIC RAVILIOUS
ABOUT 1938
See page 25

95. JUG, CREAM-COLOURED WARE WITH PRINTED DECORATION
DESIGNED BY ERIC RAVILIOUS
ABOUT 1935
See page 25

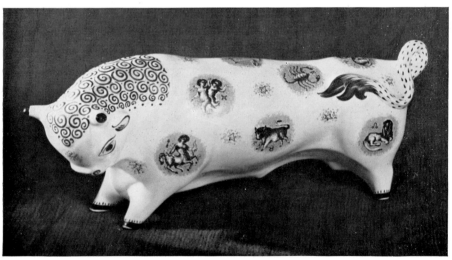

96. FIGURES FROM MODELS BY ARNOLD MACHIN
ABOUT 1945
See page 26